The STRANGEST Plants on Earth

PRICKLY PLANTS

Margee Gould

PowerKiDS press™

New York

Published in 2012 by The Rosen Publishing Group, Inc.
29 East 21st Street, New York, NY 10010

First Edition

Editor: Jennifer Way
Book Design: Ashley Drago

Photo Credits: Cover, p. 17 (right) Willard Clay/Getty Images; p. 4 Photos.com/Thinkstock; pp. 5, 7 (inset), 8, 16, 21 iStockphoto/Thinkstock; pp. 6–7 Andrew Holt/Getty Images; p. 9 (left) © www. iStockphoto.com/Rick Hyman; p. 9 (right) © www.iStockphoto.com/Robin O'Connell; p. 10 Tom Vezo/Peter Arnold, Inc.; pp. 11, 16–17, 18 Shutterstock.com; p. 12 Hemera/Thinkstock; p. 13 © P. Guillaume/age fotostock; pp. 14–15 Diane Macdonald/Getty Images; p. 15 (inset) © www. iStockphoto.com/Steve Mann; p. 19 Driendl Group/Getty Images; p. 20 © www.iStockphoto.com/ Jon Meier.

Library of Congress Cataloging-in-Publication Data

Gould, Margee.
 Prickly plants / by Margee Gould. — 1st ed.
      p. cm. — (The strangest plants on Earth)
 Includes index.
 ISBN 978-1-4488-4991-8 (library binding)
 1. Prickles—Juvenile literature. 2. Plant defenses—Juvenile literature. I. Title. II. Series: Strangest plants on Earth.
 QK650.G68 2012
 581.4'7—dc22
                                                    2010053141

Manufactured in the United States of America

CPSIA Compliance Information: Batch #WS11PK: For Further Information contact Rosen Publishing, New York, New York at 1-800-237-9932

Contents

So Many Prickly Plants 4

Thorns, Prickles, and Needles 6

A Prickly Life...8

Plants with Jobs to Do 10

Do Not Touch! 12

What Is Stinging Nettle? 14

A Closer Look at Cacti..16

The Silk Floss Tree 18

The Honey Locust Tree..20

It's a Fact! 22

Glossary 23

Index..24

Web Sites...24

So Many Prickly Plants

There are more than 400,000 different **species** of plants on Earth. They have all **adapted** in different ways to stay alive in their **habitats**. Many kinds of plants are prickly. That is, they have prickles, thorns, or needles that help keep them safe. If you have ever been caught in briars during

a walk in the woods, you know that prickly plants can hurt!

Prickly plants come in all shapes and sizes. Beautiful rosebushes have prickles. Cacti have needles. Even some trees are thorny. In this book, you will learn about some of the world's prickliest plants.

Thorns, Prickles, and Needles

Some prickly plants, such as citrus trees, have thorns on them. The thorns are **modified** stems. They can grow to be several inches (cm) long.

People often call the hard, sharp parts on roses thorns. These pointy parts are prickles, though. Prickles are pointy parts that grow from a plant's **epidermis**, or the stem's outer layer. Roses have thorns to help them hang on to and climb over other plants and objects.

Needles are another prickly plant part that some plants, such as cacti and pine trees, have. Needles are these plants' leaves. They help the plants live in hard places.

Lemon trees are citrus trees that have thorns. These modified stems grow out from the tree's branches.

Here is a close-up view of a cactus's needles.

Animals such as moose eat lots of different plants. This sometimes includes plants with thorns!

A Prickly Life

Nearly every plant needs the same basic things to live. All plants need water, sunlight, the right kind of soil, and air. They use these things and a **chemical** in their leaves called **chlorophyll** to make food. Food gives them the energy they need to grow and make new plants.

However, there is a problem. Some animals like to eat plants. Sometimes they might eat a plant before it **reproduces**. Plants have adapted different **defenses** against this. Some do not taste good or can make people, insects, or animals sick. Other plants have thorns, needles, or prickles that hurt animals' bodies and mouths.

Above: The prickles on a thistle help keep animals from eating the plant.

Right: The thorns on this plant are sharp enough to be painful to the touch!

Plants with Jobs to Do

People use thorny plants in many ways. Sometimes they can act as a natural fence. People plant thorny bushes under windows to keep their homes safe from burglars. They might plant them around a special plant they do not want animals to eat, too. People also plant thorny rosebushes because their flowers are so beautiful.

People in dry places plant cacti to enjoy their colors, shapes, and beautiful flowers. Some animals, such as the cactus ferruginous pygmy owl, use spiny cacti as safe places to build homes. Long ago, people used hard, sharp thorns as tools, too. Prickly plants are plants with jobs to do!

Above: These prickly plants are being used to decorate a garden.

Do Not Touch!

Getting scratched by a thorn or stuck with a cactus needle is not fun. Some prickly plants are dangerous, though! Australia's gympie gympie tree has been known to kill pets and livestock with its tiny, hairlike needles. These needles deliver a strong toxin, or poisonous substance.

A plant called mala mujer, or "bad lady," grows in Arizona and northwest Mexico. Its stinging needles can go right through leather gloves. The hairlike needles put a **crystal** into the skin that can cause a very painful rash. The rash lasts for many days and skin can look red, purple, or brown for weeks.

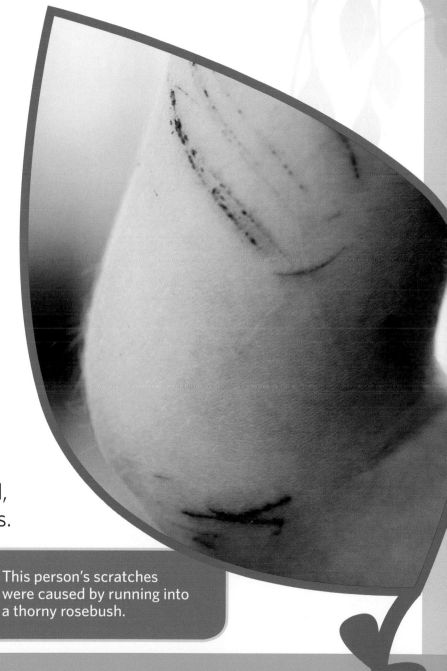

This person's scratches were caused by running into a thorny rosebush.

Stinging nettle grows in shady spots along streams and rivers, in woodlands, and in prairies. This prickly plant looks like many other weeds. Stinging nettle, though, has fine hairs on its leaves and stems. When a person touches the plant's hairs, they give off a chemical. This chemical causes pain.

This might sound like a plant to stay away from. However, this plant has been used in medicine for thousands of years. Today it is sometimes used in treatments for arthritis and allergies.

Stinging nettle is a common plant in North America as well as in Europe and parts of Asia.

Here you can see the fine hairs of the stinging nettle. Even though these hairs are small, the chemicals in them make them painful to touch.

Barrel cacti, shown here, grow in the deserts of North America.

A Closer Look at Cacti

Cacti are some of the best known of the prickly plants. Some have long, hard spines. Others have fine spines that are almost like hairs. Either way the spines are painful and can be hard to get out of skin.

The spines on a cactus are its leaves. Plants lose a lot of water through broad, flat leaves. Cacti live in

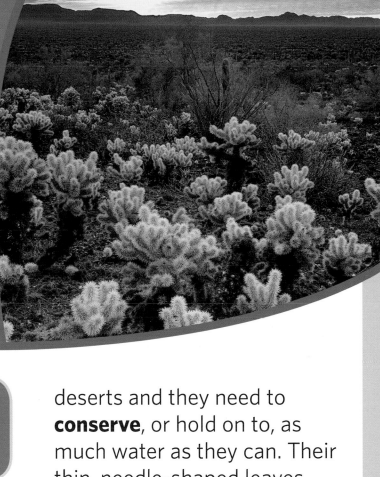

Right: The jumping cholla cactus sticks to anything that brushes against it. Big pieces of the cactus break off. When these pieces of its stem fall to the ground, a new cactus grows.

Left: The flowers of many cacti are colorful and are kept as decorative plants.

deserts and they need to **conserve**, or hold on to, as much water as they can. Their thin, needle-shaped leaves do the job nicely. The needles even give the plant some much-needed shade from the hot Sun.

The Silk Floss Tree

The silk floss tree has a bright green trunk. The trunk has chlorophyll in it, which is the same chemical that makes plants' leaves green. This chemical also helps plants make food.

The silk floss tree's trunk is also covered in prickles. These prickles store water that can be used during dry times in its natural habitat in Argentina, Paraguay, and southern Brazil. The silk floss tree has beautiful flowers. Because of this, it is grown in many yards, gardens, and parks. Its fruit pods also have cottonlike fiber in them. This fiber can be used to stuff pillows or as **insulation**.

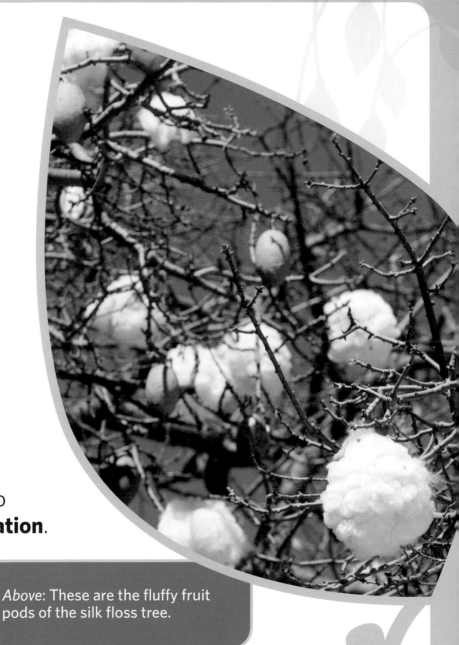

Above: These are the fluffy fruit pods of the silk floss tree.

The Honey Locust Tree

The honey locust tree would not be a good tree for climbing. It has lots of sharp thorns growing out of its branches. These thorns are generally between 1 and 4 inches (3–10 cm) long. The thorns start out soft and green but harden and turn red as the tree gets older. The thorns break easily once they turn gray, later in the tree's life.

The honey locust tree is grown in many gardens, city parks, and backyards. It is also used to make furniture and other wooden things. Its **seedpods** are food for many animals.

Above: A honey locust has the most thorns near the bottom of its trunk.

1

The jumping cholla cactus has **barbed** spines, which are hard to get out of skin.

2

The longest honey locust thorns measured were 1 foot (30 cm) long.

3

The chemicals in the gympie gympie tree do not seem to break down over time. Hairs that have been in museums for many decades still cause pain and swelling when touched.

4

A person who has touched a gympie gympie tree can still feel pain from it up to a year later.

It's a Fact!

5

Native Americans used honey locust seedpods as food.

6

Many people enjoy eating the fruit of the prickly pear cactus.

7

The gympie gympie tree is always shedding its stinging hairs. This means you do not have to touch the tree to be hurt by it. You just need to be standing nearby.

Glossary

adapted (uh-DAPT-ed) Changed to fit requirements.

barbed (BARBD) Having sharp spikes with hooks at the ends.

chemical (KEH-mih-kul) Matter that can be mixed with other matter to cause changes.

chlorophyll (KLOR-uh-fil) Green matter inside plants that allows them to use energy from sunlight to make their own food.

conserve (kun-SERV) To keep something from being wasted or used up.

crystal (KRIS-tul) Hard, clear matter that has points and flat sides.

defenses (dih-FENTS-ez) Things a living thing does or has that help keep it safe.

epidermis (eh-puh-DER-mus) The outer layer of tissue on a plant or animal.

habitats (HA-buh-tats) The kinds of land where animals or plants naturally live.

insulation (in-suh-LAY-shun) Matter that does not conduct heat or electricity.

modified (MAH-dih-fyd) Changed.

reproduces (ree-pruh-DOOS-ez) Has babies or makes another of its kind.

seedpods (SEED-podz) Parts of plants that hold seeds.

species (SPEE-sheez) One kind of living thing. All people are one species.

Index

C
cactus, 5–6, 11, 16, 22

chlorophyll, 8, 18

H
habitat(s), 4, 19

I
insulation, 19

K
kind(s), 4, 8

L
layer, 6

leaves, 6, 8, 14, 16–18

N
needle(s), 4–6, 9,
    12–13, 17

P
part(s), 6

people, 6, 9–11, 14, 22

prickles, 4–6, 9, 18

R
rosebushes, 5, 10

S
seedpods, 21–22

shapes, 5, 11

species, 4

stems, 6, 14

T
thorn(s), 4, 6, 9,
    11–12, 20, 22

Web Sites

Due to the changing nature of Internet links, PowerKids Press has developed an online list of Web sites related to the subject of this book. This site is updated regularly. Please use this link to access the list:
www.powerkidslinks.com/spe/prickly/